I0107831

Caught in the Web --

Of a Dream Catcher

Aurelio Arley Sanchez
January 2012

ISBN 978-0-578-01445-6

Author's acknowledgements:
For my parents Arley and Melba Sanchez,
my brothers Rick, (Richard) Leroy, Ken,
Clarence and Paul,
my sisters, Belma and Tina,
my daughter, Monica
and my grandson, Daniel.

Manufactured in the United States of America

PREFACE

My first attempt at writing a poem came as I tried to write in a more prosaic way an elegy for a good friend who had died unexpectedly. It is, in fact, a part of this collection. I struggled to find the right words until at last an angel took pity on my attempts at expressing what was deep in my heart. She allowed me to hear voices of angels, and I began to experience the miracle of language through poetry to express beauty, or experience emotion and healing in ways so heartfelt, so surprising, and sometimes hidden so deeply inside that only an epiphany might bring them to light. Christopher Fry said it best when he said, "Poetry is the language in which man explores his own amazement." We are all different, and yet so alike. I hope in the reading of these poems, that you might find one or two that you may like, and perhaps might inspire you to explore your own amazement. Thank you for coming here; I'm honored and humbled.

FOREWORD

I remember telling Aurelio one day at lunch that he didn't look like a good writer, but that he nevertheless was a good writer. I liked his reaction in that he wasn't offended; he just burst out laughing.

Aurelio is an emerging poet, while at the same time; he has forged a continuing, successful 36-year career as a newspaper man for the Albuquerque Journal. In "Of a Dream Catcher," his first book of narrative poetry, I enjoyed most his sensory detail and suspenseful tone, in narrative stories told, not surprisingly, in a journalistic story telling style. He paints word pictures that are raw, real and tactile: The reader can feel the barrel of a handgun, held by a domestic violence abuser, twisting "like the devil's finger" on the temple of an intervener.

In "April's Fool," a reader feels the destructive effects of hopelessness and lack of self-worth in the young son of his dead prostitute mother, who then throws himself in front of an oncoming train, convinced he'll never amount to anything more than "April's Fool."

There are bittersweet stories of found and lost love; a familiar poignancy in the wanderings of a broken heart jogging along the Rio Grande reminded of a nearly forgotten prophecy with the return of the Sand hill cranes. Then, there are stories of poetic justice and injustice: a call for prison reform "From Behind Bars;" from "eyes like grave markers gazing at dreams rotting in the sun."

There are stories of cultural alienation, as in "Aurelio's Song," in which the writer feels disconnected by his inability to speak Spanish fluently, "misunderstood by one people, unwanted by the other, pushed away by both," or in a description of cultural healing, reflected in a tense dialogue in "Mexican-American," in which American and Mexican-American discover that in the end, in their hearts "beats the same love, the same hope."

"Of a Dream Catcher" is a collection of intriguing, insightful poetry with compelling narratives framed with imaginative imagery and memorable characters. I look forward to future efforts by Aurelio, in the hope that he will continue to explore his "dreams, nightmares, and visions sifted to beauty, caught in the web of a Dream Catcher."

Jimmy Santiago Baca, author of, among others, "Martin; And Meditations on the South Valley," "Black Mesa Poems,' and "C-Train and Thirteen Mexicans."

CONTENTS

Want to See A Real Man?

I read today how a man barricaded himself
in a trailer with his girlfriend,
and before he blew her away and himself too,
he yelled to the cops: "You want to see a real man?"

You don't like Joey's; the booths are duct-taped.
You like Capo's, cozy and romantic.
But I like Joey's jukebox,
two plays for a quarter and no CDs,
just oldies with scratches grooving with memories.

Two quarters slide in but a couple behind us arc
like crossed wires,
high tension connection says he can't wait
to take her home to mess her up but good.
Your eyes cloud when I turn in my seat and say,
"Must make you feel like a real man."

His eyes blaze and smolder like embers
under the rim of his dirty black cowboy hat
perched on his head like a crow.
Her eyes are disconnected, like a broken TV.

"You want to see a real man?" he says, his tongue
burrows like a snake into his mouth.
A real man steps into the darkness to the blast
of a passing train, the bright sound arouses snakes
squirming in my belly.

"He's a psycho, *pendejo*," Joey says, "You better go,
pronto." "*Vamos*," but it's too late. The psycho's back.

The long cool barrel of a .45 is cold and heavy, and twists
on my temple, like the devil's finger.
My heart clangs like the church bell and from the jukebox,
Elvis sings "Are You Lonesome Tonight?"

Eyes lock and load and his breath is short and ragged,
like a dog hit by a car.
"You want to see a real man, *cabron*?"
We breathe our distrust and dark fear,
the air clouding of hate between us.

She begs him please, don't, and time crawls
on my skin like a spider.
He pulls the hammer down
and a real man slides back into his holster.

Real man drags her outside into Joey's parking lot,
and her screams crash back in through an open window,
but before I can stand, you push me back down again,
amazed I'd repeat "Must make you feel like a real man."

I walk to the jukebox
and fumble for a quarter
to drown out her sound.

Never Said I Was Pablo Cruise

I ramble beat and anxious, skitter like a leaf over lava rock,
a sweet city woman sings on the radio and promises
she'll wait for me. So long ago cruising Mexico
with Pablo; he asks me for one more day and I nod okay,
powerless to say no to Christmas tree eyes.

The radio blares Pablo Cruise but Pablo spins the dial.
Real rock has no horns, like Chicago, he winks, but Pablo
Cruise, he says, can come along for the ride,
my thoughts are rambunctious,
like children climbing a haystack
.
Ghosts rarely tell their tales, they are shades fading
on the Earth. Sweet City Woman's empty promises return
me to Mexico so long ago when we became *camarades*,
our friendship cemented on a Mexican weekend,
riding Metallic Blue with a name like corn whiskey
and a sound like thunder and white lightning.

Pablo rides shotgun, challenging Chevys, chiding 'Cudas,
harassing Hemis, the squeal of molten rubber
and the roar of a 351 Cleveland vanquishes Mexican Road
Warriors and Pablo beams, his golden locks whip
in the wind *como el Thor*.

Y las chulitas en Juarez bunched on dangerous street
corners, screeching parakeets with flame blue eyes
and skinny brown legs, raised skirts and silky wet
tongues, *"Oye, muchachos, Quieren dulce?
No es Caro*, very cheap."

The plaza clatters in a din *y estoy buscando el Pablo.*
He wheels around a corner like windblown tumbleweed.
He can see I'm annoyed and possessive
of the only real friend I ever had.
His speed freak eyes accelerate and he says with a wink,
"I never said I was Pablo Cruise."

Weary like a promise broken too often,
my sweet city woman still waits.
Time splashes from a shattered hour glass at my feet,
spilling blood and dreams. Death walks like a shadow,
yet we pretend it's a lie.
The old can't see the precipice; the blind can't hear the
storm, the unwell never knowing how to solve the puzzle.

I was shaken awake this morning to pay my respects.
I find you lying on a brass bed of red,
your heart bleeding from a needle full of black tar.
A cop with black mirrored eyes tosses you
in the back of an ambulance
like so many broken dishes.

Later your cold blue hands clench a rosary
and on your head a shiny new baseball cap
sticks straight up like a head stone.
The body waits, the spirit kneels afraid to go,
like a victim whose home
has been carried away by the storm.

Rosary beads chant and raging voices dance
inside my head. A smile curls like incense as I remember
the day you learned I loved your sister.
You looked in our tent and said, "What the hell are you
doing? "And your sister replied, "What the hell does it look
like?" and she slapped you so hard your long golden locks
fluttered in the wind like a young man's flag.

When your locks fell away like the leaves in the fall,
Thor died, and your eyes became his tomb.

A clock ticks somewhere on Sundays
as I search for Pablo Cruise. We swallowed miles and beer,
watched the full moon fling stars off its hip like swing kids,
living for today and wishing for tomorrow
like children on Christmas Eve,
lamenting yesterdays like lovers mourn for lost chances.

At the light a cop glares and I growl like a dog
at my own reflection. In the rear view mirror, I imagine I
see you but it's only tumbleweed.

Cruising Sundays solo, searching for solace, probing
for penance, *Como un buscador soltero*, a seeker alone.
I found a weathered snapshot of you today.
Your face was haloed in gold, and I hear myself say,
"You never said you'd be gone on Sundays,"
and then your reply, "I never said I was Pablo Cruise."

April's Fool

Pablito was born an April fool's joke.
He called his dead mom, April, a whore
and a drug addict.
"Who gives a damn," he'd say, as the train
trundled into the station, kicking up
dust like an enraged bull.

Barely 18, Pablo was a little brother
who took chances I didn't understand;
like when he stood in the road as a semi-truck
barreled at him, horns blaring
as at the last moment,
he slipped out of the way, the driver
flips Pablo the bird,
Pablo flashes back a peace sign.
"April's Fool, I'm April's Fool."

Adopted at 4, his mom found by the cops
her arm oozing Mexican black tar,
"My mom was a whore and a drug ..."
but I stopped him, "We love you, we all love you."
But Pablo built walls of silence,
piles of pain stacked
like dirty magazines in his closet.
Why do you take chances like that?"
"Because it's when I feel most alive."

The train trundles into the station,
smoke melts black eyes of a doll,
the train rumbles at 15 villainous miles an hour,
a man with black eyes of a shark,
points this way, now that way, clattering chains,
wail, whistle, have mercy, please, the children,
wail, merciless ghosts, hideous laments
of the damned, swallowed whole by the train.
Black doll's eyes, listen, they are singing, smoke chokes,
ashes swirling snowflakes, and they sing.

"My life's not worth a damn," Pablito
shouts over the roar of the train,
his smile slips across his face
like a traitor.
Just before he is swallowed whole
by the train, his eyes lock with mine,
and I see him mouth silently,
"I am April's Fool."

Exile on Main Street

Leaning against a gritty wall, she marks placid time
with a cigarette, night lurks in the gutters,
snow encircles its icy fingers around her,
clings to her hair like crystal meth.
Her hurt a harsh slit across her throat,
she lifts the lonely shadow of her face,
tosses a smoking butt into a dumpster,
passing cop blares his siren and she waves.
She feels something dying inside her,
something she never knew she had.
Her sins as tireless as the setting sun
chained by her torment and lost dreams,
an exile on Main Street.
Each evening she meanders to the streets,
nights pile like garbage behind her.
This morning, her love so despondent,
tedium conspires with pain,
and she is exiled, alone again, on Main Street.
In the pure soft white snow,
she falls gently on her back,
remembers a game when she was six,
before the city swallowed her whole.
She sweeps her arms and legs back and forth,
a snow angel appears and she rises to her feet,
watching shadows climb from gutters
open wounds across her crystal sky, and for an instant,
she believes she sees the face of God,
before she surrenders,
carried aloft in the arms of a snow angel.

Sonrisa

Sonrisa sounds like sunrise and means smile;
snow crunches under my running shoes, dawn's weak light
reflects billions of tiny stars winking up at me.
I recall today is the solstice, and your words curl
like smoke from a cedar fire. Pain swells in my heart
where I hide it and my breath paints the air misty gray.

A moment of purity and then it's gone,
the cold bronzes brittle leaves and trees,
hazy clouds arise with a swift impatience, then disperse.
Happiness is a thing imagined,
my soul runs like a fugitive in the night.

On the riverbank a company of cranes alight in a field,
strut and poke long thin bills into the mud,
sending bugs into frenzied flight.
I believe I am invisible, but one curious crane
peers at me, the rest stroll in regal indifference.

Your words like spectral spirits whisper in my ear:
"The cranes will come on the solstice and you will smile."

Flutter, flop and fall, the cranes perform
a gangling comedy of slapstick,
one slapping the other with its beak,
like Moe poking Curly in the eye.

On a sandy stage, swirling prancing delightful dancers
resplendent in the costumed dazzle of iridescent feathers
bow at last to silent applause,
performing for the smile in my heart.
A radio crashes through the trees and the cranes launch
wave after wave into a gray sky
like fighter jets in chevron formation.

Sonrisa flowers on my lips as smoke
from a distant memory drapes my heart
like an Indian blanket.
The sun lifts off from the mountain,
breathing fire on frosty meadows,
its breath warming my upturned face and your voice
envelops me like a fog as you tell me you love me.

Thunder rumbles the mountain awake, your lips
press hard against mine, my heart thrums,
frost steals my breath,
your words etched on mist between us,
"The cranes will come on the solstice and you will smile."

Sonrisa flowers on my lips
where you tucked it away so long ago,
because you knew that someday,
I'd need it.

Smell of Dangerous Anticipation

My fingertips bloody and desperate; my grip loosens,
watching Natural Born Killers marry at the Rio Grande
Gorge. The bride tosses a pale scarf from a windswept
bridge, it flutters like a death wish.
The bride wears tight white shorts over tight brown thighs,
and a smell of dangerous anticipation.

Yesterday's news show the smiling face of a boy,
released finger by finger from his iron grip
by his two best friends who toss a coin after him,
"You're gonna die, man, you can't fly,"
"For a twenty buck high you can't pay,
you're gonna die, man, you can't fly."

Natural Born Killers embrace under a roiling sky.
Jagged rocks rip away my fingernails; my grip turns to
dust, my screams crushed by incensed waters, a silver coin
glints past, falling head over tails.
Lady Luck spreads her legs for the Lord of Chance
and the languid sweet smell of dangerous anticipation.

Inside the rusty red belly of a metal culvert,
a whiskered catfish flops like a leviathan,
a sea monster the color of dirt piled by an open grave,
flopping in glassy eyed desperation, yanking slivers of air
into its pierced lungs, making a clack, clack, clack
wet sound of suffering.

Kernels of corn and a silver coin
glint from its ripped viscera,
and in the roguish water,
I can see the catfish peering at me with human eyes,
water pushing its way into the culvert
like a prison riot.
Dangerous anticipation rages in the smoky water,
the clack, clack, clack wet sound of suffering slices my
lungs into slivers of white light.

Someone pulls a plastic bag over my head,
barbed wire bloodies my ankles.
Iridescent bubbles muffle sad songs, like blue babies
bursting
at the surface, sad songs are so blue, baby.

I run my hands over the sandy cool sides of the culvert,
stabbing for an opening, screaming knives of white light
at last show me a way,
wending my way through collapsed lungs,
a silver dollar plunges past me,
lands heads up.

The sun breaks the glassy surface into billions of colors
and I can hear Natural Born Killers
walk away cursing in furious retribution,
as I step over rose petals strewn in my path,
wearing a smell of dangerous anticipation.

Little White Boots

Ten years after you packed up and moved away,
they say you've found the floor again,
your feet kicking up in little white boots,
found your rhythm, found your rhyme.

So long ago, yet your scent lingers like incense,
your eyes once so adoring frost on a sultry summer night,
captured lies chased in circles flame and flicker,
blue stars indifferent to hope,
slide to the cold edges of our sky.

I remember summer nights stoked by a full moon
and a fast car, riding roughshod like unbridled ponies,
our hearts silvery as moonlight on a mountain lake,
telling secrets breathlessly told, unbound
and flung loose to the wind.

We are our memories, we dream under tender moons
pool in mirrors.
Memories escape like ashes from a fire
until today when I heard the music,
and I paused at the rim of the last blue mountain,
at the edge of a deep blue world,
and I wandered toward the sound.

So many years after you packed up and moved away,
they tell me you've found the floor again,
your feet kicking up in little white boots,
found your rhythm, found your rhyme.

Mexican Sky

Like a dragon the sun spreads its scaly tail and flies,
as Manuelito swats at a fly shaking him awake
under the shade of the dead mulberry.
Nadine opens the door to her bar and shakes her head,
saying to Manny that it's not even noon yet.
She already knows his reply: "Its noon someplace."

He moves like the flight of the dragonfly,
hovers and dives until he settles on a bar stool
cool adobe, his soul a spider web of cracks
ready to break to shards,
shadows on his face float loose ,
the morning soft as a newborn's skin,
his eyes ebb with morning dew,
his hopes a soap bubble, fragile and beautiful.

Earlier, he felt the worms stir under him as he walked,
his death is on down the road a bit,
but now he brags he once sank a 50-foot shot
to win the basketball game,
and his laughter spills like whiskey from a shot glass.

The night yawns in an expanse of stars, the Mexican Sky
shivers under clouds wet with rain and Mannie's tears.
His only love whispers take me home,
and he cradles his bottle lovingly.

God is in the Rain

God is in the rain,
sprinkled on my face
like the kisses of a million angels.

God is in the soft
shush of snow layered
on the uplifted boughs of trees.

God is in the penitent thoughts
of condemned men
and in the salvation of the innocent.

God is love without conditions,
freely given
with nothing expected in return.

God is in the eyes of the dying,
squally fears soothed by a whisper,
a promise.

He's in the beat of a heart
of a newborn child,
holy water sprinkled graveside.

He's in the soldier's foxhole,
in the church's pew
and the dark blue mountains,

He's in the churning river waters,
the chevron flight of birds,
and in the whisper of wind.

He is in the lift of my spirit
on the dance floor,
in the exultation of love.

God is in the speckled stars
of a night sky,
in the darkness of despair.

He's in roses
picked in winter's snow,
and on Calvary's cross.

God is in places
I have never been,
or seen, he's here now.

He is in the rain,
sprinkled on my face
like the kisses of a million angels.

When Slave Becomes Master

The whip lays bare bloody bones,
skin flies like layered earth from wind, a keening
sound in the abyss, pain a lash of fire,
death impatient, scoffs because I refuse to go,
he promises he'll be back.

Ropes on my ankles and wrists constricting snakes,
hunger a brush fire unabated by the squish of bugs
in my teeth or scraps left by the master's dog.
and I wish for the day when slave becomes master.

He won't rule by fear or cage hope in a prison
and when slave becomes master, he will ask God
to forgive for they know not what they do.
Power won't be stripped from the weak,
but bestowed on the brave,
and when the soldiers demand who shall be shackled,
he will say to cast chains away, for there will be no chains
when slave becomes master.

Stench of despair, I am no better nor worse, moon
swims past like a swan, bridging time and place,
dreams of a day when slave becomes master
I rub the sun dry bones of my life
and in my unborn son's dream I bestow my own
so that when he awakens,
when slave becomes master, he will see my vision
and remember my dream.

A Yearning

Look in my eyes, deeply,
I have control now.
I love you like myself,
but I have come close to extinction
so many times and now again.

She calls and I am here,
where the air is frozen,
and I am afraid, paralyzed,
and so is she.

I could have solved this with courage
a word, but I am watching her die,
someone I grew to love,
someone who knew she was dying
by the look on my face.

And why should she lie,
when she says she's not afraid.
Why lie, Beware, she says,
but I am guilty of nothing,
except of being afraid.

I can feel her tremble.
Is there anything I can do for you?
She shakes her head no,
and yet I know she doesn't hear me,
my voice makes scratches in the air,
lightning in the summer sky.

God is metal, after all, strong and silent,
immovable, inanimate, unfeeling.
We offer grace and beauty,
grasping at things that don't matter,
blind to the only thing that does matter,
and when I offer you my dream, my life,
you smile and turn away.

When we walked in the mountains that day,
a big horn sheep came around the rock,
froze for an instant,
and then it bounds away,
It's gone, you said, it's gone.
But it will be back,
like love, hope, a yearning.

Mexican-American

You call yourself an American, a Mexican-American.
Hyphens divide and so does a leaky border.
Every time there's a crime,
it's by black or brown grime.
Don't believe me, just watch the TV.
I pay good taxes to keep you
where you belong, safely behind bars.

Brown's not a crime, you call me mojado,
but my back is dry, born here before pilgrims,
my children fight for barrios
and band in gangs of blood angry red
or brutal bruised blue,
in zoot suits and baggy pantalones,
dangling chains that bind them for life.

No such place as *Aztlan*, it died at the Alamo
with Davie and Bowie, but your tacos are cheap
and spicy, like your women.
I love a fiesta, festive and fun
but you must help me pay
to dream the American Dream,
to be like US, like the rest of US, an American.

I love America, but you steal my tomorrows,
why are my children pushed out of school,
allowed to sleep with no dreams,
called borderline, stored away in vo-ed or special-ed,
perdidos sin confianza, and I can't believe
it's a destiny que mi tata Dios ever made manifest.

We are built on unity and conformity,
diversity unnecessary, nor individuality,
just loyalty. To keep you in prison,
my taxes are high,
so high I can't buy a new SUV;
and that's just plain Un-American,
pray and work and play
like the rest of US in the melting pot.

No entiendes, I don't want to be you,
I want to be free to be me,
to speak en mi lengua,
to teach my own history,
de mi cultura, de mi gente,
and I want to honor los ancianos
who refused to melt in the pot.
Cesar Chavez said to respect
one's culture does not mean
to hold another in contempt.

Tempting visions of Aztlan,
mi casa es su casa,
Alamo is the heart of a powerful America,
pero tambien el corazon de Aztlan,
diversity breeds strength and beauty,
all of our hearts beating as one
for in all our hearts
beats the same love,
the same hope.

Angel for Hire

When he first offered me the job,
I didn't want it, too much responsibility,
and besides, I asked, why are you offering a job
like this anyway to a sometimes derelict reckless
ne'er do well who only does well
speeding way past the sound of loneliness?

Why do you think I chose you?
Exactly because you are
who you are.
Do you think those pure as divine
souls who believe they've never sinned,
or felt the hunger of bad decisions
knows what charity means?
They might know how to spell it
and they might know
where to find it in the dictionary,
but they don't know what you know.

But why can't I be an angel that can fly
or disappear or save people
from bullets on the battlefield,
or on the streets,
or why can't I make a child's hunger
go away, or why can't I stop
injustice, or evil or hurricanes?

Because we have other angels working
on those jobs, and besides your job is important too.
All I'm asking you to do is to celebrate charity,
and when you find it, send the name on
and we'll make sure charity is rewarded. Is that so hard?

I'm not looking for dramatic acts of charity
given without sincerity for show or gain,
and I'm not looking for the kind given
with expectations of something received
in return. I want the kind of charity given
with nothing expected in return,
the kind where when there is not enough,
it is given anyway, the kind where a tired and hungry
traveler afraid and in despair, is given safe haven,
kindness given without being asked,
from pure heart, with unconditional love,
though they be friend or stranger,
the kind my Son gave.

But what if people don't believe me
when I say I'm an angel, looking for charity
in a cold world, or worse,
what if they stick me in a loony bin?

Don't tell anyone, and if you do,
say you were joking, tell them
you're a poet, tell them anything you want,
just do the job, and do it well
for charity is the heart and the soul
and the beginning of all that is holy.

A Second Thought

Giant ponderosa crosses glare over a Calvary trinity
atop a sleeping tortuga, a turtle shaped volcano,
brittle leaves skitter across *malpais,*
bad lands sculpted by time and wind
into the perfect church,
always open to all and no collection plate.

Brown eyed girl wears worn shoes and worn jeans,
wends up the ancient shrine,
leaves her father's sheep at the base of the sleeping *tortuga,*
the volcano yawns indifferently as it watches a boy
arrive in his Golden Chevy.

The boy climbs *tortuga,* his black hair glistens,
he's late for practice, but coach says no worries,
the boy can spin magic with a dangling ne
and a rubber ball,
sledding on hardwood clouds like Mercury,
sinking apples into baskets, like magic.

She doesn't believe in magic; she kneels
to light an eternal flame flickering in a gusty sky.
Yellow votive candles glow and her rosary twists.
She tries to imagine her life but she's startled
by cawing overhead, beady black eyes pry
like the ladies at the church.

The boy stumbles on the turtle's back,
and she's afraid to look, but she sees just a boy
and he sees just a girl,
sonrisas flower on their faces like morning glories.

Calvary casts a cool shadow and the sun naps
como un anciano, an ancient one weary of living.
She shivers in the wind and he enfolds her,
breathing her body,
shaping her like sculptor's clay into prophecy.

Urgent guilt and delirious forbidden joy blend two souls
into one, as meddling eyes watch from above,
a black angel seeks souls in ruin.

Sunlight sifts gold on the horizon,
catches their eyes like passages to truth,
"*Me quieres*?"
and his reply,
"*Si, mi amor, con todo mi corazon.*"

At dawn a piercing white light
enters my soul, but no-one can see me.
I say I love you, but no-one replies.
A tractor engine sputters in the distance
like a second thought,
but it's too late.
I spring over badlands like a deer.

A Rose in Winter

They pray and ask me to help, in God's name.
I have to be a miracle.
They hand me the darkness, I must find light.
They ask me for proof,
I must find roses in winter's snow.
My love finds you afraid and alone,
I must give solace.
The incongruity of flight, is faith.
The stubborn souls,
agnostics and uncommitted,
justify my showing an image of Agnus Dei;
vanishes in their presence, like smoke.
There is nothing I can do.
nothing, nothing at all
I am an angel.

Dead Turtles

Wagon ruts in a river of time,
the lonely wind
plays a mournful flute,
souls gather in a radiance,
wait for a verdict of glory or gore,
the Earth shivers, shakes, tends its scars,
reddish brown rotting hulks
of dead turtles decay and shimmer
in the sun,
On the first day of spring, all I can see
are the souls of catastrophe,
behold the possessed, what I have seen
should never have been told.
the end of a man is never clear,
indifferent stars peer down
filled with hope, eternal lights and their
blue hearts ache mystified,
a man rotting in the sun, a loose shutter
claps and suddenly I remember
when I was young, and strong, when I had
everything and nothing, all I want
is to see you again..
On the horizon you beckon,
banners snap in the wind,
like the wings of angels
rustle in the radiance of destiny
and I whisper in your ear
like a prayer.

Fireworks

I was the oldest, so it was always my job
to light the fireworks,
ripping open the package
and sorting the good ones from the smoke bombs,
cones spurting sparks that we jumped over,
screaming in exhilaration at our near self-immolation.

Our dad and mom sat in outdoor rusty chairs,
sitting like royalty as they watched
us celebrate being Americans,
my uncle sometimes pushed me aside
in his drunken excitement,
holding the tip of his cigar
to the fuse, until we shouted, Run, *Tio*, Run.

But he couldn't run without the leg
he lost in Vietnam,
so he staggered till he fell,
looking up at skies bursting with rocket's red glare,
swimming in his dreams
of being a good American.

When the *ricos* moved in next door
in the house where he once lived,
fireworks boomed into the night,
long after I had picked up the smoky charred ruins
of our package of dreams
and stuffed them into the garbage can.
I used a horse blanket
to cover my *Tio*, asleep in the sand.

Smoke from a Loaded Gun

Flint strikes a sculptured flame
devours flimsy pockets of resistance,
triggers a volcanic assault of sulfurous fury,
like the smoke from a loaded gun.

I cower in a corner trembling to the screech
of a ghostly prodigy, depleted eyes watch me,
screams "Get me high, Mutha,
or you will die."

Fear tastes like the blue metal sheen
of a loaded gun in my mouth,
stands at the fork, patches of sky fly at me,
illuminate the keeper of death,
he cracks a whip of smoldering ruin,
and my soul groans at the bottom of a ditch
covered in mud and broken hearts.

Sculpted flame beckons, standing tense at the gate,
your eyes are glistening diamonds,
a tear hovers on your cheek like a pearl,
I hear your distant whisperings:
In a sunset, faith; in a sunrise, hope.

Outside my window, a candle flickers
in the moonlight, snuffed out by a thrash of wind,
hands of hurt sculpt a yellow flame
with the power to kill and no power to die,
like the smoke from a loaded gun.

Matanza Dawn

Sleepless night, dreams of Matanza morning
snip at the darkness where terror walks,
but at dawn it's held at bay,
outside in grip of cold iron,
my family works in sunny camaraderie,
roasting green chile in pungent smoky cedar,
sweet and smoky
like the hollow of a young girl's neck.

Muffled laughter to dirty jokes,
women gossip, men boast laugh and lie.
Sizzling *chicharones* silenced
in red chile and a warm tortilla.
My uncle strums his time-nicked guitar
a couple dance on a floor of dirt and hay.

Smoky cedar girl winks from the fire,
but I look away, afraid.
She knows a young boy's fear
and rubs away the blush on my cheek.
Her cold face against mine fragrant
like herbal Yerba Buena.

My dreamy vision shattered by my father's yell,
the pig roasted, now the lamb's time.
My father hands me a tugging rope,
on the other end a lamb upside down
twirling in a pirouette of fear.

I remember the serene, silent plaster lamb
lying at Christ's feet in the church,
as the practiced fatal slap
of leather beats and slaps at steel.

Fear drips freshly cut in sanguine
cedar smoke; I grip cold steel
and a meadow lark sings in the field,
melting away fright and pain,
paints the ground scarlet wet.

My father passes a whiskey bottle
and I drink, at last a man.
Cedar girl's eyes rimmed in red
and my heart sinks in sorrow
as I empty the bottle in the mud,'
the moment scattered,
no more feeling of destiny.

My father picks up the bottle
and walks away
shaking his head
tosses the whiskey bottle
high into the air.
It falls into the fire, and explodes
in a garland of flames.

Because You're Dead

Because you're dead, I'm alive.
I told you that would happen
if you could not be trusted.
I hope you like these plastic flowers,
frayed and faded in the wind,
dust devils dancing on your grave.

The rattle of chains, my wrists braced
in steel as I kneel, neither of us will escape
prayers unsaid; my knees are cut on rocks
and I wish you were here to see plastic flowers
and listen to whispered confessions
of broken promises.

Can you see me through your mask of dirt?
I want you to look at me one more time
so I can see your tears or mine will freeze
in the moment when your eyes surprised,
watched me pull out your life
on a knife covered with your sins.
If it comes down to you or me, I told you
it would never be me. If you had kept
your promise, I would never have kept mine.

Chains rattle as I pray
to Our Lady that she might curse you
and that you burn until your charred skin
sloughs away from your bones
so you can feel my tears cut you like glass.

Dimming of the Day

September's wildflowers covet the stroke
of an indifferent benevolence,
snapdragons wink heavy with intrigue,
and in the dimming of the day,
I miss your touch, your dreams, your love.

Sparrow poised on a thrusting yucca,
Shy Iris sensuous and silky
like a woman awakening.
Gilded rock roses gather like children
for the ice cream man.
Butterfly weeds detonate
in tangerine anarchy.

September's wildflower lifts her face
for a morning kiss,
and prickly pear curls in jealousy.
Blossoms sway to crickets' chirp,
honeysuckle dances with the breeze,
imaginary eyes search in softness,
Virginia Creeper boasts plump purple berries,
but promises no wine.

In September's wild graces
lie a conspiracy of waiting,
austere and forbidding,
yet reckless daring finds beautiful intrigue
wild and free in the dimming of the day.

I Don't Think of Her Anymore

I don't think of her any more,
except when the stars wink at me
from a cold black sky,
my heart at the helm of a drifting ship,
shivering in cold blue diffidence,
suddenly I remember how she shivered
in the wind, my warm breath playing
in her ear like a song.

Her kiss lit a fire, small and easily doused
at first, but it was not doused,
growing each kiss, raging out of control
like the sun, the hot and sensual sun,
and when I touched my lips,
my fingers burned, the fire consumed my heart,
leaving white ashes strewn over the wreckage.

I know I loved her. I know she loved me.
I don't like to think of that night
under a star-domed sky,
the wind nudges me closer,
insistently, until I hold her in my arms,
and our eyes converge in a full moon,
both halves glow like embers.

When she loved me, her eyes were huge,
swallowing me like an ocean
the smell of her sweet breath in mine,
her mouth sweet and wet, my fingers wrapped
around her hair, tangled by the wind.

The wind, warned me night after night,
the night will be gone, until one evening
when it became a nightmare
of desire and deprivation,
until at last I shouted to the wind,
the hateful wind to stop,
but the heartless wind tormented me still.

I don't think of her anymore.
I know I loved her. I know she loved me,
but her eyes don't see me anymore.
The wind is breezily quiet,
tired of taunting me,
my soul strangely resigned,

when I say I don't think of her anymore,
except on nights like tonight,
when the flame of her kiss returns me
to the deep hollows of my sorrow,
her eyes in the sky become jagged
points of light
shining on the treachery
of a broken heart, and I drift like a ghost ship
into the cold black night.

When You First Appeared

When you first appeared,
I was swept away by grace and flowers
in the flow of your western skirt,
your tap glide boots sliding on slippery
wood floors, and when we walked
later in a moonlit field,
God was there listening and smiling.

When the stars faded and moon mountains melted,
the moon returned each month every month,
and though we were lovers in grief,
you could feel my arm around your waist,
pulling you close in the dance
for the rest of our lives, but the music stopped,
and the dance died.

When you last appeared,
singing of tires on an open road
drew me to a mountain town,
where you, as if time had stopped,
beckon me, bringing the dance,
I saw the phantoms gazing at us
from the crumbling adobes,
residing unseen with the living,
the golden blissful autumn light pounds
the red rocks, making a sound like pounding surf,
and the phantoms gazed from the red rocks.

Our moment scatters like grains of sand,
the moment scatters in the wind
slips through my fingers, but nothing
is ever extinguished, or forgotten.

Our souls unlocked from hellish red rocks,
the desert fills me with its hot dread breath,
desire rises from my wounded heart,
beware, sweet heart, listen to the notes
of a song, watch them soar on the wings
of a metal Eagle, suspended in time
in the village art store,
look in its eyes, the black dead eyes.

Look at the Eagle overhead
casting a shadow on the wood bridge,
a crossroads, and when you next appear,
tell me how to ease the yearning, tell me how to douse
the burning, and when my peace heart sings,
tell me why my blissful dreams end.
Tell me now, why a perfect moon has no light,
tell me why there is no hope,
tell me how to forget you,
tell me how a moment's love
can make a perfect world,
tell me why you return only
to say you remember.

Not the Same Man

This man who playfully tosses my little girl
up reaching for heaven,
her eyes searching for God,
to the sound of wind chimes -
is not the same man.

This man wearing kind gray eyes
and a rumpled baseball cap,
spinning my little girl
to peals of laughter -- isn't the same man.

He's not the man who abducted my mother's
oil portrait, a likeness her friends
said made her look "*como la* Liz Taylor,"
always making her giggle.

He's not the same man who scoffs
at a portrait
painted by an artist
on a Mexican street corner
who places a beauty mole on her chin,
como la Marilyn, for no charge.
The artist accepts humble gracias
from a woman who collects love
like an old man
collects aluminum cans.

This isn't him, not the same man,
with a cool black curl in the middle
of his forehead, like Elvis.
He's not the same man who carried
his rifle hunting rabbits on the *llano,*
my brother and I piled into the back
of our Ford Fairlane,
and we flew tail fins up and windows down,
bouncing over *bordos*, bumping over rocks,
our boy hearts beating like the wings of captured birds.

This isn't him, he's not the man
who coolly shoots his rifle at the hostage portrait,
and then glared at the screen door
where my mother watched and waited
like a widow of war, both casualties,
she lowered her eyes and turned away
as if from a grave.

This man who tosses my little girl high
reaching for heaven,
her eyes searching for God,
to the sound of wind chimes -- isn't the same man.

Stealing Beauty

She gave one last secret look,
anxious eyes searching,
and she twists like a rose stem over water,
searching for promises she can't find.

Reflections of September,
scent of her hair hangs in the air
like morning rain and fresh cut rosemary,
her cold toes curl against mine,
her brown eyes hide,
her body reflected in the moon's
artistic glow, cold night air a silent sentinel,
and I like a thief,
stealing beauty like apples,

in awe of her dreams,
promises captured and stored,
for when she awakens,
bewitched by a scent of lilacs.
of rain frosted sycamore
in the cold night air,
and I like a sentinel
illuminated in full moon's glow,
watching as I steal beauty
like apples. and she as innocent
as sleep, searching for promises
she can't find.

Juniper Winds

Volcanic blood courses through red rocks,
beating to the rhythm
beneath snow white cliffs,
reflected in the icy illusion
of a full moon, like the ebb and flow of healing springs
bubbling to the surface,
souls torn asunder reborn in the swirling water,
and through Juniper winds,
I hear an echo, lonely and weak,
a white wolf peers from its amber leafy shelter
licking wounds from vicious battles
won for love and fear
while her pups frolic
blind to the terror.
Juniper winds whisper
and echoes drift like forgotten thoughts
locked in red rocks,
brown brittle leaves clapping
in desperation flutter to the ground,
while drums thrum in red rocks.
White wolf lopes unseen, seeing all,
she pads in amber forests,
howls a plaintive welcome to a crescent moon,
souls reborn in the healing springs
of volcanic red rocks,
their thoughts bubble deliriously to the surface,
brittle brown leaves cling and now pale
and in Juniper winds and the howl of the white wolf,
flutter to the grateful ground.

The Deer

The deer drifts in panels of sunlight,
a still life painting,
suddenly bounds away
on legs made of springs.

Wind leafs through my body
like the pages of a book,
reading the stories of my life,
laughter and sorrow,
no remorse.

Roses painted like ladies of the night,
hopes of love,
willows' shade invite me to tea.
Sun rises, its warrior helmet
breaks onto the battlefield,
princess moon trails in gossamer gown
sprinkling silver shadows in marble snow.

In the clear damp chill of morning,
the Earth waits to charm. and to be charmed,
rosy sweet scent of flowers and soft fur,
crumbly aroma of rain scented dirt
Trembling leaves mark my path,
the snap of a twig signals
exuberance of life witnessed
in the heart stirring leap
of the deer.

Violence of Our Rage

Ditch waters in the acequia shimmer, bitten by the sun
on the backs of highway workers, skins burned brown,
    children scamper like mice from a yellow bus,
and my brother sees me waiting, the bus lifts off like a
            dragon belching black smoke.

Along a ditch bank choked with bamboo, cracked beer
    bottles sail in circles like battleships, we sat under
a cottonwood, and in my heart I yearned for something,
    to be a little boy, but I knew that time had gone
            as soon as I was born..

At the train yard I listen for the train to the distant
    wail of an old woman crying, the engine hisses
like a snake, taunting, tempting me to go, and every day
I felt the power, but I could not though under my breath
            I said not now, but someday.
                        ,
When I opened the door I heard the ugly word
    "*Mientes*!" screamed again and again,
        the word opens a gash over my eyes
            filled with acid. I asked someone
    the meaning of *Mientes*, but she asked me why,
        "Has someone called you a liar?'

I shook my head no, and hurried away.
A snake shedding its skin wants nothing
    but to be left alone, emerging with no trace
of the old skin, that made them ugly, small and afraid.

Demons scurry about in my heart and mind,
my dreams sloughed away like skins of
snakes baking in the sun, the old woman
of the river eats the hearts of children,
drinks their dreams like wine.

My brother always at my side in the violence
of our rage, when we haunted broken streets,
played poker and pool, stalked the chaste
and chastised, who stayed always at a distance,
fearful and fascinated
like rabbits to the coyote, my brother always
at my side learning the power of unity
living our stories in the violence of our rage.

I am still here and so is my rage.
I could have escaped many times, and as I
look through the slits of my life,
bloody hopes thick and crusted.
A candle flickers in the dark, a life waxing
on rosewood, an altar with candy skulls
and time simmers on the wasted night.

This morning I brought out my gun, loaded,
and in the blue metal sheen of the barrel
I saw my reflection, told to go back home
though I was here long before Plymouth Rock.
In the blue metal sheen I saw my uncle
who lost his home after he lost his leg
in Vietnam. I saw my daughter who gave up

her golden dreams to work at the golden arches.
In the blue metal sheen, I saw my friends
die young, addicted to hopelessness,
and the rage seethed, boiled under my skin.
I clutched my magnum and readied to leap
into a simmering cauldron of hate.

But then at that instant, at that very instant,
like a cooling summer rain,
my little grandson walked in, hand-in-hand
with his new little friend, my grandson brown
as the wheat chaff and his friend white as the lillies,
and I saw into his future that there was no need
for violence nor rage, and I put my own away,
prayed and hugged them.

When they asked why I cried, I smiled and replied,
"These are not tears, little ones, just a cooling rain
washing away my sins," the swirl of the wind
and the river filling my breath with cool
and there I saw God, smiling at me,
I felt suddenly a hunger to know him,
"Love the world as you love me,
love me as I love you."

That Time in the Morning

My eyes open at that time in the morning
when I can hear her song playing dreamily,
the sun peeks shyly on a brittle winter dawn,
dappled sunlight spills through a window
and I wish I could be by her side.

The air cool and crisp like the snow
on trees outside her window,
an angel's song plays.
In her heart she knows she's come so far,
her love stowed away for the trip,
until that time in the morning
when there is nothing to hide.

Her song finds joy in freedom,
borrowing a memory
and mixing it with mine,
and as I play her song once again
I can see her flying beyond the sky
chasing her dream.

Her song rises in lazy curls of smoke
from my cup, framing a wintry scene outside,
vast plains stretching to mountains
draped in a blanket of white,
her song soars over frozen fields
to the notes of a distant piano
playing dreamily in the aching hollows
of my heart, at that time in the morning.

The Lady Wore Red

The Lady wore red, slow dancing
to a love song, her scent fresh cut juniper after a rain,
Simply Red holding back the years,
I ask her to dance with me for the rest of my life,
her lips on mine sweet rounded fruit,
and my heart breathless heart runs like an unbridled pony.

The Lady wore white, communes with angels
at a mountain sanctuary where miracles are mined
from Sacred Mother Earth, her hands clasped,
her hair catches halos of gold in the hushed light
and my heart glows.

The Lady wore green, walking hand in hand
with me in an emerald forest, scent of pinon and pine
sweetly mingling in an embrace
atop swirls of marble
over walls of crashing waves.
Awakened early to burning ceder,
kisses sparling fireworks.

The Lady wore blue, neon glitter
in a City Different, sashays
like a devil with a blue dress on,
"magic in the touch of her dress,
silk and satin, leather and lace,
black panties and an angel's face."*
Black-nyloned legs wink at me
through veils of blue.

The Lady wore gray, my soul sinks
in the crash of her sacred heart
dropped from a high shelf,
a priceless vase of shattered dreams,
lay in shards at my feet,
reflecting tears of bittersweet surrender.

The Lady wore black, grieving
for a man tall and good,
who knew how to love her,
who knew how precious her love,
how fragile her heart,
yet he was led away before his time
by a heartless harvester.
my own love helpless to heal her.

The Lady wore red, swirling lace
and bouncing curls frame
her dancing brown eyes
under a Harvest Moon,
Her heart beats alive again,
her love of life dances in the splash
of her smile again
and I smile for her, from afar.

Spanish Ponies

"I was Spanish before it was cool,"
Joty says to the little Spanish pony he kisses
on the nose.
The little horse shakes its mane mightily
as if to agree, excited and bright as a newborn foal.

Joty brags on the horses like they were his children,
and I guess they are.
He tells of a race he won on his Spanish horse,
riding the wind like flash and thunder in a storm,
a bigger stronger horse breathing
dusty puffs from flying hooves
of the speedy steed that attracted no bets,
and little faith, except from Joty.

Brought here in the holds of galleons,
carried with no cares conquistadores and braves,
playful and funny as puppies,
powerful and brave as a mountain lion,
loyal as familia, agile as a gazelle,
resilient and beautiful as red sandstone.

Pushed over cliffs for being born free,
shot by hundreds like the ill-fated Buffalo,
chased too close to extinction,
but coaxed back a day at a time,
stabled by the Bacas under the sun and misty moon,
under heaven's clouds and star-domed skies.

Look to the mountains of Zuni,
where God still lives,
where the ponies still cast a wary gaze,
stamp their wanderer's hooves,
rear and spin and prance like children
on Christmas Eve.

Watch them run like Hidalgo across mountain meadows,
their bodies flowing in perfect synchronicity
like the notes of a favorite song,
tails held high, lifted by Brother Wind
where freedom reigns
and now so too the horses.

See them assemble in the morning light,
now grandly called Spanish Colonials
as the First Horse of the Americas,
and you may hear a pony neigh,
"I was wild and free before it was cool,"
and Joty and Virginia
y *todos Los Bacas*
can do nothing but look at the little horses
and smile.

Techno Spiders

Oscillating lights spill electric paint,
techno touching vanilla scented dancers indecently,
willing dead presidents cling to red satin
and black lace,
techno pulsing to thigh high leather
and black stiletto heels.

Wild frenetic strokes tapped on a hardwood floor,
oblivious to the crack of guns,
a figure outlined in chalk on the sidewalk,
grasping bloodied dead presidents,
his legs akimbo and hands clasped,
his final prayer unanswered.

In the shadows, willing dead presidents
change hands to the clash of war drums,
pressed by unseen sweaty palms
and stuffed away with a wink
and a knowing smile.

Syncopation prattles like a machine gun,
pleasures of willing dead presidents
sought by kings and thieves,
makers of dreams and broken promises,
pasted side by side
on starry, starry nights.

Steamy techno dancers in black satin
and red lace,
kicking to long cool speakers,
a sea of undulating bodies
peppered by strobes,
oblivious to the inferno.

Orgasmic laughter fills the desert air
from a sultry temptress
pulsating in her smoky neon ecstasy,
sirens howl through the streets,
dangerous songs bristle with tension
fraught with fear.

Willing dead presidents
skitter like scorpions over the sand.
Techno spiders dance,
terror glares from behind a black hood,
ears shut to the anguish of mothers,
deafening growl of metal dogs
running in the valley
of the shadow of death,
repeating again and again
there is nothing to fear.

Amazing Moon

Amazing moon glides in a cobalt sky,
shadows reflect walking dead
in a prison of craters and cheese,
golden bells of an Aztec goddess
glimmer with tears, banished
forever for falling in love.

Ring-shaped moon burnished bronze
like an ancient piece of jewelry,
glimmers like a wish.
glows temptingly like an antique doorway
to a long abandoned castle,
a passage to a princess, an escape unseen.

We share a kiss secreted in a passageway,
chills course through my body,
unleashing a lustful zest,
her lips sweet rounded fruit
an Aztec moon brims with rapture,
as I whisper in her ear,
"Amazing moon, makes me dream of you."

I pause at the entrance unsure,
helplessly drawn like steel to magnet,
swimming in the sweetness
of her being, reflected in the moonlight,
sharing shivers of delight.

Goddess of golden bells
imprisoned by custom,
ruled by desire,
disowned by disgrace,
languishes in the dead light
of a prison for one.

At dawn's amber blush,
an arrow sings across an argentine sky
as a Goddess runs to freedom,
her chains slip away
her arms bind me close
as she whispers in my ear,
"Amazing moon,
makes me dream of you."

Aurelio's Song

Me acuerdo when I was in grade school
and my teacher called me
from across the playground;
She asked me if I had spoken Spanish.
Overcome with guilt and fear,
I confessed y *la dije que si.*

I knew recess was over when she led me
like a prisoner of war to a little room in the back,
where I faced a wooden instrument of torture.
I begged *por otra chansa,*
pero la maestra said it would hurt her
more than it would hurt me,
and it was for my own good, *tambien.*
A loud swat and laughter
from another room started a fire.

I went back to class to learn
about the Constitution, the Alamo,
and Pledge of Allegiance.
My tongue had been cut out,
sin sangre ni cuchillo, with no blood
nor knife, and the fire burned.

When I stood with cap and gown
y *mi abuelita's* old eyes brimmed
with pride, I could only smile at her
from beyond the invisible wall
that kept us strangers.

Y *cuando mi patron* asked me
to translate at work
and I shook my head no,
I heard him mutter,
a Mexican who can't speak Spanish?

Al fin, I decided I'd reclaim the stories
de los ancianos y *de* mi *cultura,*
but it was too late.
Language is better learned young.
Un dia, I was fishing in Espanola
and I asked *un buen hombre* for a good spot.
He looked at me like I was *pendejo*
and I heard him say a *sus amigos,*
es manito, though I was not his little brother
and my blood ran as brown.

And when my own daughter
for a school report asked me how to say,
"I am Chicana and I am proud."
She saw my dismay when I turned away
con verguenza.

Misunderstood by one people,
unwanted by the other,
pushed away by both.

Me acuerdo quando mi maestra
cut out my tongue,
starting a fire that still burns
como un infierno.

Aztec Warrior

Aztec warrior bronze and hard
like a tarnished penny,
walks wary and wounded by wars
that left him scarred and bewildered.
He calls himself Aztec Warrior
though he never heard of Montezuma.

Street fighter and barroom brawler,
his fists like uncut diamonds.
He poses in stiff muscled irony
in front of a '57 Chevy, an illusion
of metallic strength without humanity.

Pain follows him like a starving dog,
leaving a trail of dread and agony.
He keeps in his pocket
a faded photograph of his lost love
and another of a brother cut in two
by the steel wheels
of a merciless freight train.

He takes off his shirt at the river,
deep scars course on his back
like a den of snakes.
From his father's leather belt,
he says, to make him a man,

to teach him survival in a pitiless world.
I am Aztec Warrior, he boasts, none can defeat me.

Yet he pushes a swing and delights my daughter
her laughter fills the air like wind chimes,
and he pushes her once more,
revealing the soft heart of a prickly pear.

A stranger approaches and he bristles
like a copperhead.
but I remember his tenderness
with children and I ask him
who showed him kindness,
where he learned love.
"When you weren't afraid,
When you were my friend."

Anticipation of Death

Anticipating death, my temblor soul
like a coward hides,
I wonder what will be said
or if anything will be said at all.
I wonder if death will be man or will she surprise,
will death bring pain or will pain end.

I remember as a child learning life ends,
the moon and sun conspiring to lie
a cold dread fell upon my immortality.
My heart thrummed with fear of the knowledge
I was already dead, and so too
were all born of mud dried to dust.

Anticipating death, I wondered if I die today
or tomorrow the end of time,
better to know or better not,
relentless whispers driving me to madness
until I at last I saw another path.
Anticipating death, two paths broke off,
one into the yellow woods, the other well-traveled,
I watched a maple leaf picked from its branch
where it soared and fluttered in the joyful wind
until it clapped to the ground in helpless desperation.

Stars blink indifferently from a velvet canopy
watch us with rapt fascination at life's brevity,
breath a silent prayer of thanks
the cosmos knows no ruler Lord Time.

Our lives withered and brown play
a bony rattle, shocked, we are frozen
in fear, the sun and moon whisper
there is nothing to fear.

In the still of morning, in the quiet still
of morning, the sun gaily waits for the sound
of children laughing, hearts breaking,
turning my life over and over
in my hands like a treasured heirloom.

Your marvelous golden grace
nearly lost like a treasured heirloom.
Forgotten and stored away,
brought out to dust and to contemplate,
its golden grace resplendent in the light.

Something Happened

Something happened to me when my name changed,
bestowed by my grandfather sung like a song,
tossed in a trash heap because they could not trill an R.

Something happened to me when my Dad
turned away from a restaurant with a sign in the window
"No Mexicans or Dogs."

My grandfather wipes away my tears,
whispers the sacrificial lamb
replenishes the sun, the gift
returned as light and life.

Music notes gather like birds on my uncle's guitar,
the aroma of tortillas and roasting chile
cooking in cedar smoke, my *tias* cook *carnitas*, a warm
tortilla envelopes me like a hung,
and something happened to me.

Tears of countless broken hearts wash clean
the walls of my jail cell, names and dates
tattooed on the walls, from a window the world
outside is close enough to touch,
and something happened to me

and when I learn a bullet from a cops' gun
shattered my friend's heart,
his only crime to say no, he will not be turned away.
his body growing bullets and vengeance
in his desert grave.

Something happened to me,
as I thought of my own grandson
who would rather
play bad guy than cop.

This morning outside my window,
the snow left a shimmering blanket,
of pristine white, bunched in spots
like a treasured heirloom
carelessly dropped,

a snowflake wets my tongue,
wistful and cool,
like an angel's sweet breath,
and something happened to me.

Birth of a Goddess

She'd never been to a big dance,
never been invited.
Called Tomboy by her brothers for so long
she felt it was her name,
but tonight her smile gathered sunshine
and sprinkled it on her shoulders,
electric light to the sound of music.

When I led her onto the floor,
her body resonated like a violin,
playing a beautiful song
I had never heard before,
my heart thrummed from her touch.

Friends since first grade,
she beat me in a foot race,
then said it didn't matter.
I loved the taste of rainbows
she pulled from the river,
and I basked in the sunlight
of her red hair.

When bullies cornered us
and kicked away my books,
she swept into a swirling dervish
of flying hands
and feet that I joined by her side,
unleashing my best Apache war cry.

Later under a warrior's moon,
giggles and laughs burbled like elves
over our bellies, and I told her
she was the best girl I ever knew,
and pretty too.
Her cheeks burned bright red,
like embers in a Christmas fire.

I took her home after the dance,
coasting on the twilight,
the blue stars still affirming
the bond between Heaven
and Earth, and I asked her
if she had a good time.
She kissed me,
her lips dancing on mine,
giving me prickles of thrills.

As I watched her
go through the door
flying inches over ground,
her smile a pretty red ribbon,
I wondered how or what
had transformed her
into Goddess.

Ramble

Desire inflames spangled lips,
red pumps stir sparks
on a catwalk windy with stars,
a galaxy dazzled by black nylon
and red garters,
energy pulses from a comet
rambles closer, and in the shadows
planets swirl amid a taste of sugary pears.

Tingles on your lips linger on mine,
collecting heat, even your eyes are meteors
pulled by an irresistible force
I can't resist,

bending your body like a knife half opened,
your red lips flame like in comet's tail,
and a desert wind murmurs dangerous promises
whispered in soft sighs
sparking fires in the heavenly bodies
out of control.

Saturn and Gemini witnessto our unrequited love,
lonely winds with a scent of lilacs,
your soft skin draped by a satin scarf of secrets.
My disheartened desire pulses in a dark universe,
a comet celestially alone.

Venus & Circe

Satan created man,
God so pitied man
he was moved to give man a soul,
but this created two faces,
one of good and one of evil,
each veiled by the other.

Inside anarchic Iraq, a man steals a golden mask
to help his family escape.
Lady of Warka forces him to don her stolen mask
to behead his wife and seven children.
Warka at War moves men to behead other men
in the name of God.

Faint pulse of a natural born killer rises
in a beautiful woman dressed in white
for a wedding of dangerous anticipation.
She embraces her love at an altar
of pumice and brimstone,
spider cracks spread over a wedding vase
of antiquity, a kiss sparks a conflagration
in bloody Rome, while the Emperor fiddles.

Circe proffers a chalice of wine,
red moon sails on a ghost ship
in Jove's starry court,
while in the moon's shadow,
a lost garden turns to stone,
a brother slain by his brother,

both bleed on the dark side of the moon.
Circe lifts her chalice, her breasts swaying.
Circe sings softly, weaving an illusion of innocence,
the tempest raging and sailors dreaming
of when they were men.

Eyes of Venus, stars created
by the union of Heaven and the Sea.
Hooded eyes peer into a black hole,
voracious and greedy, witnessing the birth
of a new universe, consuming itself,
emerging on the other side frosted with stars
and smeared of lipstick.

Venus and Circe hurtle toward a perfect circle,
inviting and dark,
wet and fraught with mystery,
Constellations converge,
seducing brute force
like the instant
before the Big Bang.

Venus slips into her gown of gossamer,
Circe dons her mask of gold,
and at the edge of a deep dark rim,
like ravenous animals tensed for the kill,
they flutter noiselessly into an unsuspecting sky.

Mystery of Your Art

In the viewfinder of your camera, a rose
blossom shivers, unsure
of your love or your intentions,
not the sincerity of your look,
nor the mystery of your art,
will soothe its fear,
like yourself, reserved and mysterious,
scanning the beautiful scene, layers of colors
of green and brown and blue,
topped by a grayness of subtle movement,
the light
like heaven, and when you give
such a gift of mystery, settling at last
in silence, you enfold
in my arms shivering against a wind,
warm and soft, fragrant
like the blossom, young again
your brow furrowed in wonder,
some happy memory in the lines of your life,
in a moment's intimacy, a glance
all knowing, anticipation of love,
in the viewfinder of your camera,
you see something not yet in focus,
a masterpiece not yet imagined..

Laugh Again

We fly over ground my grandfather walked;
he was tall, slender and strong,
like a rail, they say, and he laughed
often and long, and he made others laugh,
but he died before I could store that sound in my heart.

I am called Grandpa now and we fly into the wind
on my bicycle.
My little guy is strapped in a pouch
on my chest so his arms and legs
are outstretched like Mighty Mouse
on his way to save the day.

My heart pedals furiously, his tiny arms circle tightly
in blinding arcs like a hummingbird,
my feet pushing against gray
gusting breath in our faces,
our hearts fill with flight and we ascend.

We soar over alfalfa fields and deserts
my grandfather walked,
over an ancient cottonwood
where he whittled toys for me
from driftwood and he was pleased,
they say, when I smiled.
I wonder if he will know me, and share my laughter.
I know babies can't remember, but then he turns in his
pouch and he laughs, and for an instant,
I hear my grandfather laugh.

Carrie's Dream Catcher

Ringlets of gold grew in Carrie's hair.
She never liked it, she tried to straighten it
with stuff from the store, but I liked it.
Ringlets seemed to light her way in the dark
and gathered sunlight like a dream catcher.
I never told her that, though I said it was pretty,
and for an instant, I think she liked her hair.

But then her mom came in; she had blonde hair too,
her hair was long and straight, every hair in place.
Her mom always yelled at Carrie, please do something
with your hair.
Her dad had curly black hair, wild and untamed,
like Carrie, and only the wind combed it.

Carrie played basketball like Magic,
Johnson that is, and one night when she scored
so many I lost count, her ringlets
stayed tight and bright.
She told me her dad scored more
when he played for the state champions
in '51, and when she showed me his team picture,
he wore short shorts and we both laughed.
But then he died, he was just 42, Carrie was 16.

The gold in Carrie's hair seemed to turn to bronze;
the light left her face, shadows there I hadn't seen before.
She blamed her mom when her daddy died,
but I didn't think that was fair, and I told her so.

She walked away without a word.
I thought she was going to college,
but she went to Dallas instead,
never kept in touch.
I asked her sister, "How's Carrie?"
and she'd shrug her shoulders
and walk away.

I never asked anymore about Carrie.
I watched a women's' basketball game
on TV and I thought I saw Carrie,
so I pressed my face against the screen,
but it wasn't Carrie.

I heard on the grapevine
Carrie's living on the streets
of Dallas, I heard she gave up
looking for a job, so she got a job walking
on the streets.

I wonder if the men she walks
with like her hair.
I wish I had told her
her hair was like a dream catcher,
only instead of dreams,
it catches light from the sun
and lights up the dark.

The Day the Birds Stopped Singing

I was in the back of our Fairlane reading the Sunday
comics when I heard a thump, like the sound a dog
makes when it's hit by a car.
I was reading Dagwood and checking out Blondie
wondering what she saw in him when I heard the screams.

It was my grandmother making a sound I had never heard
before, like La Llorona, the witch lady who killed her kids
and then went looking for them all over eternity.
I got out of the Fairlane, my grandpa ran to the road
where something just a little bigger than a dog lay
crumpled, blood streaming from its head, leaving a growing
pool of red.

My heart began to flutter and crawl like a moth batted to
the floor.I ran toward the crumpled shape in the road,
but my grandfather stopped me, and yelled to my grandma
to stop screaming and come and get me away from there.

A motorcycle lay on its side by the side of the road,
it's engine still running,
the front wheel still spinning,
catching the glint of a beautiful April morning.

My grandma took me and my brother inside
where she made us kneel at her altar and pray
to a plastic Jesus and a ceramic Mary,
begging God please don't take our little brother away.
But our little brother did go away, and the next morning,

I heard the birds, the sound that always made my heart
danceeager for the songs of a new day.
Then I remembered my little brother,
and the birds stopped singing.
I yanked at the knife in my heart,

but it was immovable, like the sword in the stone.
My eyes follow the clouds floating in silence,
gray and pregnant, changing shapes,
suspended in time.
Every morning when I wake up,
I listen for the birds,
but the birds don't sing anymore.

Secret Scream

A young man's silent shadow leaks moist red
on black rocky asphalt, a perfect profile
soaked indelibly in the rock of Highway 47,
young black hair braided and broken in two,
leaks sticky red, leaving a shadow in the rock.

In the quiet morning,
your boots are perfectly formed,
down to untied shoelaces the only sign
of the violence of your final moment,
like the first time, ripped
from your dead mother's womb
20 years ago, the secrets of your anguish
carelessly tossed to the wind.
How in such a short life did you see all causes lost?
Depressed in darkness, helpless to fight back,
tears torn from your face
like the wind and rain in a hurricane.

Among your pathetic heirlooms I find a notebook,
filled with pentagons, unpaid bills and poems:
As I read, I can hear your voice,
defiant and angry, "Sitting all alone on my own,
drowning is infinite, you will be me, just like me."
I shut the book and shudder,
but I am compelled to open it again.
"I see you, you see me, I am you,
you are me. I write a word, I speak a verb,
I hear a sound in the future."

The sound is mine as I turn the pages:
"Seeing nothing, something happens
secretly, discreetly, they steal you away
and never give you back.
I see you, I know you,
I knew you'd read this."
The book slams shut,
but its spell is unbroken:
"Silence, Can you hear it?
Can you smell it?
Someone at the door dressed in black
selling emptiness, "Want to buy some?
I hope you don't remember me."

But I do remember you, I remember us,
your brothers and sister, your dad and mom,
we brought you in from the storm
and into the fold when your mother died.
I remember too that we stayed behind
and tried to hide from an ambush of bewildering fire,
embracing life as you did death and your secrets.
You could have broken your silence,
we could have led you from the dark,
but you closed yourself around yourself,
though just beyond the rim, we waited.
Sunlight streams over your shadow,
giving up nothing. Soft snow falls, blanketing the silence
and covering in frozen pristine white
a perfect profile in the rock, the secrets of your anguish
locked in a breathless scream
nobody heard.

Civil War

A family lays its son
to rest in a closed casket
so his mother can remember
his beautiful face
before it was blown up
by a roadside bomb.

Protestors across the street
wave flags and chant
a dead soldier is a good soldier.
Biker vets hold flags high
and roar their Harleys
so the family can't hear.

We must stay the course
to avert a civil war,
the President says,
but it's too late,
the war is here.

Born on Halloween

Born on Halloween yanked from the womb
into a cold brutal world by *La Curandera*,
chanting fills a room of smoke
and my mother's screams,
duel with the shrieks of the wind
outside our adobe, born with hope
for love and mercy, but it wasn't long
before I learned not to kneel
nor to look in a mirror
afraid there would be no-one there.

Born on Halloween with a mask,
children teased, laughed never knowing
how deep the wounds, how ugly the scars.
pero la curandera promised me healing
in her black bag of spells, and I remember now
when I learned not to pray nor to kneel.

As a boy, risking punishment
of a leather belt, I looked through
a key hole, *La Curandera* called
to our L shaped adobe, to protect us from evil,
her ancient parrot perched on her shoulder,
it turned its beady eye toward the key hole
and screeched, and shrieked, *La Curandera* massaged
on my grandfather's body, feverish near death,
my grandmother's rosary clicked somewhere
in the dark behind him, "*Padre estrous, perdona nuestras
ofensas,*" *Dios te salva, Maria, bendita tu eres
entre todas las mujeres.*"

The parrot's shriek broke my trance;
the bird crashed from wall to ceiling, frantic
to escape something I lied later I did not see,
the witches cat erupted in its own freakish panic,
and the old woman tossed the toad skin
as if it burned her hand into the fire,
bursting into flames and plumes
of black smoke, from which rose a black
and gruesome apparition, licking blood
from its lips and it grinned, so hideous
I had to avert my eyes, and when later
the old woman asked me what I had seen,

I could not answer though the terror
my eyes reflected a hunger of death,
a cackling bony visage, dreams of bleached
bones resting upon a lonely beach,
in a world without love or hope, I saw a crippled
soul walking upon the brittle landscape,
alone for eternity, with no love nor hope.

I ran out into a deathly cold night,
and knelt on the same frozen
ground where died many others before me,
their whispered warnings wafting
from the *camposanto*, warning me,
night after night,
remember, time is short, time will die

I can still see my grandfather that night,
his brow dripping, brought back from death
so near the precipice,
his voice shaking, begging me to tell him
what I had seen, my terrified silence
making him cry, asking me what I had seen,
my silence making him cry,
and the old woman warns again,
love and mercy sometimes come too late,
sometimes not at all.

I can hear the wolf's padded prowl outside,
I can hear it bay to a full moon, waiting,
born on Halloween, I pause
to find at my feet shards of remorse,
wasted emotions, and cast away dreams
strewn about the wreckage
of my life, of blackened hopes,
and I vow I will never, no, I will never
kneel again.

A woman in black wails at the river,
her cries curdling my blood,
she asked me, have you seen my children,
her face wracked with pain and guilt,
my eyes had to break away,
"I killed them so they could be happy,"
I killed them only so they would be happy,"
and when I looked up again,
she was gone, but her wails still rang in my heart.

The black wolf at last trains its red eyes on me,
trots and breaks into a run, it's tongue
lolls as it reaches breakneck speed,
leaping, its fangs aim for my throat,
but *La Curandera* stands before me,
the woman who brought me into this
cold dark world one Halloween night,
she grabs the wolf by its throat,
and with powerful hands in one swift motion
breaks the wolf's neck and no whimper.

La Curandera spoke urgently, angrily at me:
"I will soon bring you into the world, and when I do,
you will **never** abandon hope,
you **will** kneel, and you **will** believe,
and I looked into her eyes of fears
and tears and newborn blood,
and I knelt and prayed I would find
love, mercy and hope,
and that I would find it in time,
born on Halloween.

Penitente

The devil's eye fixed on the penitente,
a ghost burns inside him like guilt
Rain srinkled on his grave like Mary's tears,
but there is no-one here to pray for him.
He told me once there's nothing to fear
in life except to die alone.

Rosario erected a Calvary shrine atop El Cerro,
a giant turtle shaped volcano long dead
inside its blackened shell, tortured in a desert of sin,
paralyzed in brimstone.
The old penitente in his last days was a tractor
started with a crank, strong and useful once,
later just a red rusting hulk
performing penance with a fifth of Tokay.

He danced with the devil on Bayou marble floors,
fought on frozen Belgian turf as Panzers devoured
his best friend who begged him to fire his rifle,
at last his amigo banished to hell
by the spray of shrapnel, screams of betrayal
frozen in the brittle cruel air.

The penitente bears his guilt like a cross
he carried every day to the top of the mountain,
a coward's burden he could never shed,
his amigo haunted him nightly asking why
he left him to fight alone against an infernal
monster swabbed in a swastica squealing of fire and steel.

I stand alone at his grave, my sorrow
crawls over my skin like spiders,
the penitente's soul scoured with self inflicted whippings,
his penance earned, but never paid.
Under the red glare of the devil's eye,
I touch sprinkles of holy water on his grave,
a wraith rises from the dirt, screaming.

Eagle Feather

You will find my Eagle feather floating
in the waters of time, light glints
from the stream at Taos, casting shadows
of gray and black,
like a prison gate,
melting my hopes
like ice sculptures in the sun.

The water sings like a waterfall,
emerging from the frozen brown Earth
light glances from depressions of icy white,
smoke escapes from many
chimneys, *chile ristras* flash red against
brown adobe walls,

In the distance I can hear the drums
and the soft swish of feathers getting closer.
Yellow stalks of frozen wheat lash blue doors,
timeless river carries my feather like a dream.

Tiny bells jingle from belts and moccasins,
dancers move like a covey of doves,
and in the glint of white arcing light,
I see a young warrior reach into the river,
clutching my feather, bridging time,
the sun bursting through bare aspen beauty.

Smoke trails into the sky, reaching high
feathery clouds hover
over pink dotted mountains,
solemn deep prayers in the dance
unlock the gate of time,
and a warrior's anxious vigil ends,
the warrior reaches to his father
and rises into the smoke.

Her Black Book

I found the black book,
a slim letter sized log with a black vinyl cover
like a monk's robe, the word "Record"
embossed in faded scratched inlaid gold.

My fingers slid over pebbly leather, invoking my
grandmother writing in candlelight,
poems and prayers of loss and love, sensing a cutting knife
of guilt and desertion, but no anger for God's will.

She had resolved though often hard to see, that his will
had design, even when the heart of her long cherished
esposo, the heart of her loving husband stopped
like a watch dropped in water.

Yellowed faded pages stained with coffee and tears,
words in Spanish of pain, farewell, solemn portraits painted
by a suffering Lady, vestiges of light in her eyes
dabbed away by the night.
Adios Esposo querido, she wrote, *Adios companiero fino*"
on the next page, a lament of the loss of her son, who
survived being born too soon, and later a poison drink,
a fall from a roof and bucked by an unbridled pony, missed
by a treacherous treasured rifle that backfired.
The hooded man in black would not be denied.
And when his harvest was done,
the boy hunter was found by a meadow lark's song,
and a coyote lapping at his life spilled on cruel Highway
47, late for a date with the Class of '64.

Life is hard, she wrote, but we must be strong and keep
our courage, and our prayers as well. Her courage and faith
finally spent, she's a shadow tiny and gray, her smile
singed by sorrow, faded by fear.

The final page of her black book disclosed
she had departed in terror,
alone at the brink,
holding tightly to her book,
she asked someone only she could see,
Robber or saint, and no reply.

From Behind Bars

From behind bars, they call out like cats,
time frozen on clown face clocks striking midnight.
When the lights go out,nightmares begin,
out of cities, out of God's pure country,
out of ghost towns, out of neon's glimmer uptown,
out of fear, out of anger,
out of bitch, out of bastard,
out of mother's poisoned heart,
out of empty pockets,

from jars left ajar,from traps lightly sprung,
from a shiver of cold,
from crying alone face to the wall,
from no light at dawn,
from eyes like grave markers
gazing at dreams rotting in the sun,

out of dead men walking in circles,
out of boys become men
or not, their empty shells tossed in a pile,
from the stench of denial,
from a lunatic moon,
from no reason to rise,
out of lives torn asunder.
They come, without end, out of blindness,
out of vengeance is mine,

from a beast feeding on spirits,
from a need for closure,
from lockdown, from lights out,
from everything under control,
out of rehab is for quitters,
out of an eye for an eye,

from a blackout can be a busy little devil,
out of time served,
and still imprisoned.
out of cruelty, out of unusual,
out of what might have been,
out of lonely, out of time
from the color of dirt piled by a grave,
out of today is the first day
and the day after yesterday,
from behind a curtain
of faith, from a bursting of hope
smothered behind bars.

Nobody Cares

I heard a migrant on the bus the other day
say *que estaba excitado porque la esposa y los ninos*
were coming to join him.
He would not have to send his money
he earns tarring rooftops in the summer.
I heard him say he tried hard to find a good *jale*
in the vallage where he grew up,
pero los ninos were crying
from the pangs in their stomachs,
so he paid a coyote to bring them across,
stuffed like animals in the bowels of a rolling furnace.

He told me he spent two months in a county jail
when he got here, *y alfin* they let him go.
I heard him say it wasn't hard to find work.
He needed work and they needed it done.

I heard a cop say they found a big truck spilled
on the highway, it's tires blown out and the driver
no where to be found, its cargo of people spilled
like tomatoes on the hot asphalt, gathering flies.

I heard the cop ask his supervisor if the mostly women
and children dead should be moved off the road.
some were bloated in the heat, others gathering flies,
but the sarge shrugged and said, "No, nobody cares."

I heard a newspaper editor ask, "Do you think anybody
cares about 30 migrants perishing to death in the desert?"
'Nope, nobody cares," his colleague answered.
"They do care about $3 a gallon gas."

I heard the man on the bus ask why
the bodies weren't moved off the road,
then I heard him scream, and he began to run
to the corpses rotting in the sun,
"Mi hita, mi hito, mi esposa,"
and he ran out tears streaming,
embracing sun-drained corpses
on the blistering pavement,
all that was left of his family,
chanting over and over,
"Si, me importa, I care, Si, me importa."

A Piece of Paper

"No te preocupes," I said to my mother
who thought me crazy
for signing a piece of paper to go to Iraq
and fight in a war *por los Estados Unidos.*

I told her it was the best way,
the fastest way to get a piece of paper
saying we were *Americanos,*
eligible for all the comforts and rewards
of living in a place where my great grandfather
once walked, before Manifest Destiny
declared him an immigrant
in the land where he was born.

Displaced and condemned to live
in a ghost town
where all the men had disappeared,
the lonely women opening empty mailboxes,
occasionally getting a handful of dollars
for *frijoles* y *tortillas,*
waiting for word when they could be reunited,
in a promised land.

I made friends in Iraq even after one man
called me brown nig***,
and later when I shot the wild eyed Iraqi
who tried to take his life,
he never called me anything after that
except good Marine and friend.

The President of the United States promised me
a piece of paper that would make me *Americano*
if I went to the front lines,
and I was so close, just a few days away,
but the Iraqi who shot me didn't know, didn't care,
becoming *Americano* was his nightmare.

I would have liked a 21-gun salute,
some of my *compadres*
from the war were there,
but the mayor of my town said no guns,
so they lay me to rest quietly,
the only sounds my mother crying softly

When the man from the U.S. Embassy
in a blue suit wearing dark glasses
walked up to my mother and gave her a piece of paper,
her eyes spit venom and she crushed the paper
Under her heel, "Congratulations," it said,
"You are now a citizen of the United States of America."

Nine Inch Nails

A nine inch nail split the top of my hand
between third and fourth finger, tendons writhe
like snakes, electrocution flashes, eyes roll in ,
excruciation, a mallet slams into shards of pain
the mallet poised to strike again.

My other hand immobile over a wooden crossbeam,
jack booted heels crush my neck as the mallet descends
at the speed of another scream escaping from the crush
of my bloody chest.
The mallet pushes the nail at the speed
of sound striking unquenched lust for blood.
Never fear how you will die
my grandfather said and if you do, never speak of it
or your fear will be repeated each day
without hope.

Hell is not of demons, nor pitchfork
nor lake of fire, but the death you most fear,
will be your own private hell.
I did not want to die on the cross.by crucifixion,
but I dreamed I dragged a mammoth cross
of wood and bones up the steep sides
of my private Calvary, lashed and pierced
at every step by sword and spear,
and at the crest to wash away my sins,
I lay on the cross full of remorse,

wearing exhaustion of despair,
pricked back to life by the first penetration,
a heavy spike slammed
through the top of my foot to cross,
screaming with the second,
the spike ramming through my other,
begging the Roman
to please stop, crying unabashed,
anything to please stop,
let them all be damned,
but the Roman just smiled, his face
becoming my grandfather's telling me
again and again, never fear my own death
for it will become my own private hell,
pain rips into my body like hollow point bullets
for the rest of time.

For a Man like Me

For a man like me, it's never hard
to lure a woman to her shallow grave,
like this one, her pretty face
looks up at me
from behind a mask of dirt.

It's not hard for a man like me
to charm and lie she's beautiful,
to tell her I have a job for her
earning double
what she makes en la *maquiladora*,
sweat shop in Juarez, and she believes me
como una puta pendeja.

"You don't have to do this, please,
don't do this," she begs like all the rest,
crying and begging as if I care.

She's from Chiapas
just two weeks at the *maquiladora*,
where there are no security people
to keep a woman like her alive.

The factory bosses, *los hefes cabrones*,
y *los pinche Americanos*,
all they want is money; money
is all they want.
No guards and no place to stay

for a woman like this
make it easy for a man like me.
Esta muneca, this little doll,
Estella, a pretty name
for a pretty woman
handcuffed at her wrists and ankles,
whispers terrified in my ear,
while in her pueblo, her mother cares
for her two little girls,
y *como llora*, like a baby
when she remembers her Angelita y Dolores.

She doesn't know a man like me
never moved by a mother's tears.
"Please, I have children."
and I slam my shovel to break her face
and dig in peace.

Just 19, no more worries now
that a man like me takes her worries away.
stalked like the wolf,
caught kicking in killing jaws.

Laid in the cruel light of a cold moon,
her face becomes my little sister's face,
and I pray a *mi Tata Dios*
that she will never, please God,
never let her meet
a man like me.

A Prayer, a Promise, Placitas

Sunlight floods the Sandia Mountains,
light blasts from hill to mesa
wind a pounding surf,
changing scenery, remnants
of an ancient sea
painted in scarred rock, captured
by the painter's palette,
a prayer, a promise, Placitas.

Wild horses cast a wary gaze,
ears forward, tensed muscles
uncoil
in perfect synchronicity, tails held high.

Summer meadows ablaze, colors
riot, purple asters gather like children
waiting for the ice cream truck.
Red dahlias burst
in tangerine anarchy,
Grape vines promise wine,
but none for me.

Scarlet roses lay siege
to an elderly church
wrapped in an old woman's
brown adobe coat, her back bent
from so many years knelt
in prayer, snapdragons outside
wink heavy with intrigue.

Walking on a dusty Placitas road,
the wind leafs through my body
like the pages of a poetry book,
re-telling the stories of my life.

Autumn veils a conspiracy,
austere and forbidding,
reckless daring and beautiful intrigue,
pristine white snow,
and the passage of the white wolf.

In the damp chill of Spring,
a sweet smell of rain scented dirt,
a sense of renewal
mirrored in ageless waters
swift, frothy rips breaking
over rocks
of Las Huertas Creek,
a prayer, a promise, Placitas.

Essence of our Autumn Tale

I have seen the aged givers of destiny flicker,
entertained at my speckled imperfection,
that all I know of great-soul immortality
is, "There, there, the Big Dipper," Ursa Major
reaches out as if to say there is no wisdom
beyond man's understanding.

A solitary tear of sterling hovers on your cheek like a pearl
the mountains disappear against a backdrop of velvet,
hope like a smoking lamp flickers and fails.

To have watched you ride on the side
of a rugged mountain,
to have shaded your eyes, ignored the din,
sultry and sunny, shaded and jaded.
soft in sweet repose, freshly cut in orchid's pose.
your eyes ever searching, smiling.

Silence can never hide the honor
of those lovely nights when dreams
hovered out of reach,
a sweet crisp fragrance wafts
in from your open window,
unbroken promises
laid away for another day.

A glance back at a Persian cat
asleep on a windowsill cedar framed,
a wild horse ears forward, muscles tensed,
barely seen amid pinon and pines,

and you at the piano,
reading a borrowed book,
a still life portrait of eager beauty.

I have heard the gift of water glance
from polished pebbles of a river bed,
I have seen the magic sunlight
in a dappled field of flowers
where I found you,
alone, awaiting, our bodies sweetly mingled
in silken discovery.

Memories may never fade
caught in scent of timeless trees
heavy with rain in our Autumn dusk.
Angel, merciful angel, lifts me now
from this lonely valley,
let me see mountains heavenly with fog,
flowers breaking gates with color.

To have watched a full moon
from beyond your coyote fence,
to have heard the coyote
sing its summer song,
to have counted stars
in ancient light,
to have felt the beating
of your heart
sounding softly
a rhythm of rain.

I have heard the silence of faith
in your breathless whisper,
I have felt the cold hard stones
beneath my feet,
poised at the arch in your garden,
stepping through it, a last kiss,
a long embrace,
a look back,
enshrouded in morning mist,
these are for us
the essence of our Autumn tale.

Star

If you want to be a star,
you'll need a fan.
If you want to be a cool car,
you'll need a fan.
If you want to be a star
in a cool car,
you will need two fans.

www.ingramcontent.com/pod-product-compliance
Lightning Source LLC
Chambersburg PA
CBHW051838040426

42447CB00006B/587